TEACH YOUR CHILD TO READ

A Mommy + Me Coloring Book

Written & Illustrated by
Elisabeth Forde, M.Ed.

Acknowledgements

Thank you to my angel, my favorite, my gift from God - Lilly - for your patience and support of this book. Love you to the moon and back and around the universe, Mommy.

Cover Art by Manuela Guillén.

Teach Your Child to Read: A Mommy + Me Coloring Book
©2024 by Elisabeth Forde. All rights reserved.
Second Edition: April 2025

Find more early reading tools at School.ReadingGardenClub.com.

Table of Contents

Page

TEACH YOUR CHILD TO READ

Welcome Letter

Dear Parents/Caregivers of Early Readers,

An **early reader** is a young child starting a lifelong reading journey. Early readers learn the alphabet sounds and how to blend sounds into words. Early readers should be taught using an intentional and structured literacy pathway. The early reading stage is usually taught across 3 school years (from kindergarten to second grade). Reading is taught at home when a parent believes their child is ready.

How will "Teach Your Child to Read: A Mommy + Me Coloring Book" help you?

This tool goes beyond teaching the alphabet song. In fact, you don't have to teach the alphabet song. I taught the alphabet song as a calming song for my little one, but it did not help her learn to read. This fun coloring book models playful ways to connect with your child, instruct at home, and guides you to the best early literacy practices. You will know exactly which sounds to teach first and how to best engage active children.

This phonics scope and sequence is designed to support parents who want to teach their child to read at home. The coloring book is informed by the science of reading research that I use in my practice as a dyslexia tutor, and my experiences homeschooling.

How should you use the coloring book?

1. Read the parent guidance on the left pages before, during, or after the right page.
2. Read the right pages aloud to your child like a series of short stories. Encourage coloring, but it is not required.
3. Ask your child to repeat the letter name, keyword, and sound.
4. Start at the beginning even if your child has had early reading instruction.
5. Go outside and make connections to the real world and nature.

Each vignette or short story should be retold to help your early reader remember the keywords. Keywords help the early readers remember new sounds.

If you want more detailed guidance, learn more about the early literacy resources at School.ReadingGardenClub.com.

Happy Reading fams!

Elisabeth Forde, M.Ed.

Your Reading Teacher

Sounds vs. Letter Names

Prioritize teaching sounds over letter names.

Letters are picture symbols of basic sounds. Letter names help early readers identify correct spelling, but it will not necessarily lead to sounding words out.

There are 26 letters but 44 sounds in English. Sounds are auditory. Letters are visual representations of sounds. What can make teaching reading in English challenging is that the same letters can be rearranged to form patterns that represent different sounds.

For example, 'y' can say /y/ as a consonant or /ī/, /ē/, /ĭ/ as a vowel. Depending on the location of a y in a word and the letters around it, its function and sound will change.

Hello! This is Big.
Welcome to the sound garden.

Keyword phrases

Reading and memorizing the keyword phrases is the magic sauce. This is a visual and auditory support for early readers. Repeat these keyword phrases as often as possible.

1. Say letter name.   a
2. Say keyword.   apple
3. Say sound.   /a/

b

Big is a bumblebee.

b bumblebee /b/

How to Teach - The Methods

THIS <u>METHODOLOGY</u> REQUIRES YOU TO MAKE A MINDSET SHIFT.

☐ **<u>Teach sounds not letter names</u>**
Focus on teaching sounds not letter names. Knowing sounds helps a child sound out letter symbols to decode. Letter names help a child to spell and are not necessary initially.

☐ **<u>Keep it short</u>**
3-6 minute lessons depending on the child's age and interest.

☐ **<u>NO sight words</u>**
Do not teach sight words yet. This may be the biggest mindset shift. Teaching sight words without teaching decoding skills leads to guessing.

☐ **Speech-to-Print is just as important**
Mastery also means a reader can hear a sound and point to or name the correct letter symbol by sight 100% of the time.

☐ **Location, location, location**
Establish a place to be more intentional about literacy. Store sound cards and a timer here. Call it a "sound bag" or "reading nook." Make it special!

☐ **Keep reading aloud**
Keep the joy of reading alive for your child by continuing to read aloud.

☐ **"Good readers..."**
This is the time to teach and model good reading habits. Correct with positive affirmations. *Good readers sound out unknown words.*

☐ **Connection is more important than outcomes**
Young children value the time together with caregivers, more than skills.

☐ **Invite others**
Welcome other caregivers to support your child's reading journey.

Big sits on an apple.

a   apple   /a/

How to Teach - The Methods

THIS <u>METHODOLOGY</u> REQUIRES YOU TO MAKE A MINDSET SHIFT.

Start with self-reflection. What did it feel like to learn to read?

- ☐ *How did you learn to read?*

- ☐ *Did you sound words out? Were you asked to memorize whole words?*

- ☐ *Do you think you learned to read effectively or was it hard?*

- ☐ *Do you enjoy reading? Why or why not?*

<u>PRO TIP</u>:

★ Letters are initially just squiggly lines to early readers. Letters may not look different from numbers to young children.

★ Learning to read is not as natural to a child as learning to talk. Children may not care about the importance of reading, yet. Find joyful ways to engage their interests and motivate them. Try to understand why an early reader will continue to prefer you read to them.

★ Sounding out or blending is not a skill most early readers observe. Early readers generally observe adults that do not need to sound words out. Some early readers may be resistant to sounding words out as a result. Ask your early reader questions to find out if this is the case!

---

g

A girl eats the apple.

g   girl   /g/

How to Teach - The Framework

<u>Basic Lesson Structure:</u>
This lesson structure should be expanded as the child masters additional sounds and syllable patterns. Use the "Reading Action Plan" template in the Appendix to document your lesson structure.

Sounds (1 minute)
- Use sound cards to review sounds
- Use the coloring book keywords to review sounds, re-read the vignettes or short stories
- Use real world objects to review beginning sounds

Decoding Words (1-2 minutes)
- Practice blending 1-3 words based on sounds the child has mastered using the wordlists pages in the book
- Encourage the early reader to read words they can in the vignettes

Games (1-3 minutes)
- Play a game that supports phonemic or sound awareness
- Play games throughout coloring book and via the game list in the Appendix

bag

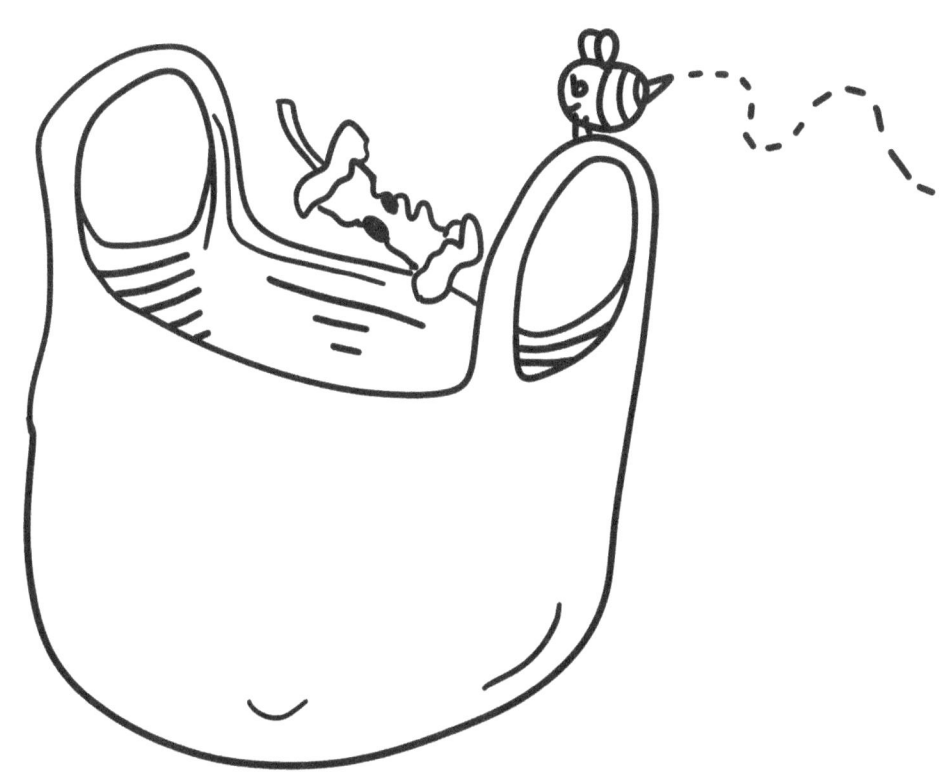

The girl throws the apple
core in a bag.

The Overall Plan*

Start at the beginning. This coloring book covers the Basic Code and Early Blending. An extended scope and sequence is available in the Appendix.

1. The Basic Code	
Use the basic code on the next page to teach your child 3-5 sounds at a time. Teach consonant digraphs after you teach one sound per alphabet letter. Teach the concept - "short vowels" and "consonants." Using sounding out loud strategies, teach your child to blend these sounds together into CVC words.	Short vowels *(a, e, i, o, u)*
	Consonants *(b-z)*
	Consonant digraphs *(ch, th, wh, ck, sh)*
2. Early Blending	
Using sounding out loud strategies, teach your child to blend these special sounds together.	Consonant blends, no new sounds *(br, mp, cl, st, dr, etc)*
	Glued sounds *(am, an all)*
	Glued sounds *(-ng/-nk sounds)*

Draw your favorite toy.

t   toy   /t/

The Basic Code
Alphabet Sounds with Keywords

Vowels:

a - apple - /a/
e - egg - /e/
i - iguana - /i/
o - otter - /o/
u - up - /u/

Consonants:

b - bee - /b/
c - cat - /k/ *
d - dog - /d/
f - fish - /f/
g - girl - /g/
h - hill - /h/
j - jump - /j/
k - kids - /k/ *
l - leaf - /l/
m - map - /m/
n - night - /n/
p - peek - /p/
qu - quail - /kw/
r - run - /r/
s - snake - /s/
t - toy - /t/
v - vine - /v/
w - well - /w/ *
x - fox - /ks/
y - yawn - /y/
z - buzz - /z/

Another letter(s) makes the same sound.

Scope and Sequence

	Sounds
Group 1	b, a, g, t
Group 2	s, i, p, k, c
Group 3	f, o, x, qu, j
Group 4	d, e, n, r, l
Group 5	h, u, m
Group 6	v, w, z, y

tag

Play
Sound Tag!

When "tagged," say a letter name, keyword, and sound to escape.

Cultivating Lifelong Literacy

What literacy activities do you already do with your child?

- ☐ Morning, naptime, bedtime read alouds
- ☐ Children's book clubs
- ☐ Weekly library field trips
- ☐ Book wishlists (instead of toys)
- ☐ Read environmental print (signs) with your child
- ☐ Talk about the authors and illustrators of their favorite books
- ☐ Attend author talks for children
- ☐ Create multiple reading nooks for your child
- ☐ Alphabet song
- ☐ Play with letter toys
- ☐ Make books/scrapbooks with your child
- ☐ Model reading your own books in front of your child
- ☐ Reread favorite books
- ☐ Find books with characters that reflect their identity
- ☐ Trade books with other families
- ☐ Read outside, parks, playgrounds
- ☐ Create a bookshelf for your child only
- ☐ Find non-fiction books on their passions
- ☐ Encourage your child to learn to read in another language
- ☐ Pack books instead of toys for the car
- ☐ Play with dolls, so they read and learn to read
- ☐ Play with toy vehicles, so the drivers read signs
- ☐ Point out beginning and end sounds in words in daily life
- ☐ Go on sound hunts inside and outside
- ☐ Practice writing letters with playful materials
- ☐ Coloring books about learning to read

s

In the garden,
Big has a snake friend.

s   snake   /s/

Speech to Print

Reverse Sound Drill

A reverse sound drill is when the adult says the sound, then asks the reader to repeat the sound and point to the correct spelling of that sound at the same time. This tests your child's phonemic awareness of the sound (not just recognizing the picture of the letter).

Easy Sample Script:
★ **Parent:** *Say /w/.*

★ **Child:** */w/*

★ **Parent:** *What says /w/?*

★ **Child** points to the letters "w" and "wh" (*child can also say the name of the letter for more advanced readers)

★ (***Parent:** Is there another way to spell that sound?*)

i

Big also has an iguana friend.

i   iguana   /i/

How to Teach - Blending

The most important reading strategy for an early reader is blending out loud. When a reader says all the sounds in a written word aloud, the reader listens to the sounds they made in order, and then pushes the sounds together into a spoken word.

For readers struggling with the more traditional blending, try different types (additive blending or onset/rime blending).

☐ **Use touch to teach blending**
Young learners learn by doing. Reading feels like an action when they are touching a tool or tapping their fingers for each sound. The touching also focuses their attention and brain on the sound they are making.

☐ **Teach 1 syllable pattern at a time**
There are 6 syllable types. Children should first learn the closed syllable pattern or CVC with short vowels. This coloring book will only focus on teaching closed syllables (described in detail in later pages).

☐ **No guessing**
Guessing is an ineffective strategy even if it is based on context clues like pictures. Do not encourage this bad habit.

☐ **Stretch the vowel aka continuous blending**
Vowels are the meat of words. Without a vowel, there is no word.
Example: c - aaaaa - t

p

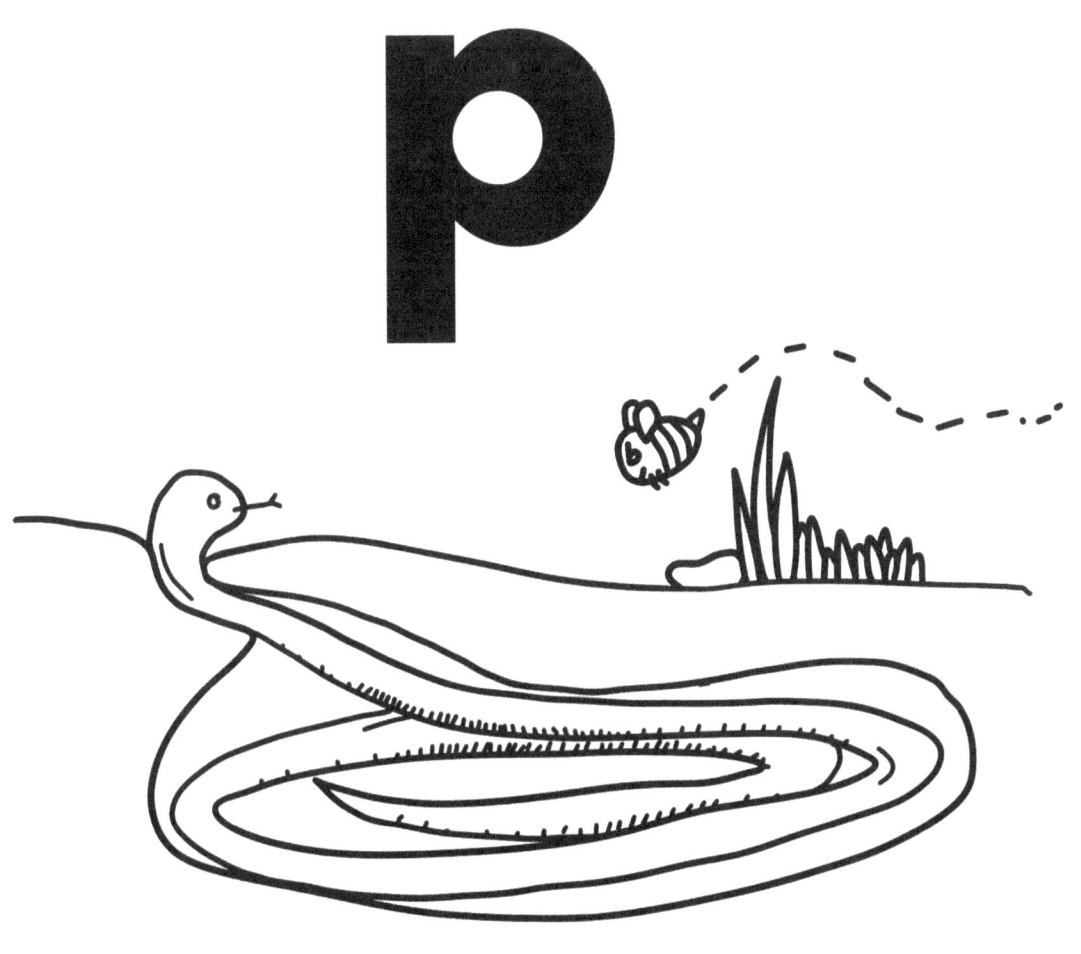

Snake peeks out to say hi.

p   peek   /p/

How to Teach - Blending

PRO TIP:

★ Eye tracking and focus is a prerequisite to successful blending.

★ Some people might say your child is not "ready" if they struggle with eye tracking and staying focused. Sometimes being ready is situational and not a permanent state of being for a young child. A child may not be ready after seeing their favorite uncle walk in the room with their favorite toy in his hands, but they may be "ready" after a routine of quiet reading before bed becomes a habit.

sip

The animals sip water from a pond.

How to Teach - Finger Tapping

Finger tapping is a hands-on method of sounding out words and blending them.

The reader finger taps each sound (not letter) in order, starting with the thumb and pointing finger. Once each sound has been tapped (one sound per finger), then the thumb is run across the tapped fingers to help the reader blend the sounds together.

PRO TIP:

★ Fingers are a free tool, but some young children may not have the fine motor skills to utilize this strategy yet!

Additional hands-on tools:

☐ Spinny Blocks with books for early readers

☐ LEGOs or similar plastic blocks

☐ Letter magnets

☐ Montessori movable letters or sandpaper letters

☐ Bananagrams, Scrabble, or similar letter-based game

Play
Sound Knock Knock!

Adult: Knock knock!
Child: Who's there?
Adult: /__/
Child /__/
Adult: What says /__/?
Child: [spells letter name]

Vowels + Consonants

The most important concept to memorize after understanding letters are symbols that represent sounds is vowel/consonants. There are 5 vowel letters in English. All other letters are consonants.

Vowels
★ Vowels are sounds made with our mouths open.
★ There are 5 vowel letters in English. All other letters are consonants.
★ There are 20 vowel phonemes or sounds in English.

Consonants
★ There are 21 consonant letters in English. And 24 consonant sounds.
★ Most consonant letters only make 1 sound, but some make more than 1 sound depending on the context. For example, 'c' says **/k/** and **/s/** (also known as a hard c and soft c).

PRO TIP:

★ 'Y' is the sometimes vowel, which can be confusing for early readers. Teach 'y' as a consonant initially with this coloring book. 'Y' is usually a vowel when seen in the middle or end of a word.

★ Use color coding when possible to differentiate between vowels and consonants. Use one color for vowels and a different color for consonants.

---

k

Kids play in the sound garden.

k   kids   /k/

Troubleshooting

qu
All 'q' words are followed by the letter 'u'. Tell your child these are "buddy" letters or are "married," so they always stick together. The 'u' next to another vowel is also a clue to help children that get the p/q confused.

PRO TIP:

★ Read aloud silly picture books about 'qu' to help your child remember (like *Q & U Call It Quits*).

Repeat keywords for difficult sounds
Repeat the keyword and sound before reading a word - every time.

Example:

Reader says keyword phrase first, e - egg - /ĕ/. Then the reader sounds out a word with "e" like "deck".

Whisper phones
A plastic tool that helps amplify the sounds the reader hears when sounding out in their ear.

C

Kids chase a cat around the pond.

c   cat   /k/

Troubleshooting

Letter reversals - b/d/p/q

Many children get b/d confused. They also may get p/q confused. This does not mean they have dyslexia, rather it is a normal struggle. Lowercase b/d are binary options. That means if a child identifies b/d incorrectly, they can immediately guess the other letter. This does not force them to learn how to discriminate between the 2 symbols.

<u>PRO TIP</u>:

★ Use the "thumbs up bed" graphic below to teach your child how to quickly check if a letter is b/d. Tell your child to use their thumbs up to visualize the word "bed" and determine the correct letter sound.

★ Use the "thumbs up bed" **<u>before</u>** a reader begins to sound an unknown word out. If the early reader does not learn to check beforehand for the correct sound, they are continuing to guess and the graphic is not needed.

---

f

The green fish swims in the pond.

f   fish   /f/

Troubleshooting

Be Patient. Teaching reading is not a race, but rather a long game.

Early readers...

- ❏ May not want to sit at a table.

- ❏ May not even be able to sit still.

- ❏ May have difficulty keeping their eyes focused on a word. Remind them this is part of reading!

- ❏ Struggle with blending initially.

- ❏ Sound like robots. It's okay to model the word for them once they do the work.

- ❏ Need to sound words aloud, but will fight you because they never see/hear you do that when *you* read. Sounding out words aloud is the only effective way to learn how to read.

A brown otter wades by the fish.

o otter /o/

6 Syllable Types

The syllable information in the table below is provided for parent information. Early readers do not need to master all 6 syllable types yet. Early readers will master closed syllables only in this coloring book.

It's important for early readers to understand that many words are made of multiple word parts. Discuss the key reading concepts on these syllable pages with your early reader when you believe they are ready.

		Letter pattern	Vowel sound	Example words
1.	Closed	VC	1 short vowel	if cat chick
2.	Vowel - Consonant - e	VCe	1 long vowel + silent e	file ate stole
3.	R - controlled	Vr	1 vowel changed by r	far born fur
4.	Vowel Team	XX	short vowels, long vowels, diphthongs	ee - teeth oo - look igh - light
5.	Open	V	1 long vowel	hi be sty
6.	Consonant - L - e	CLe	silent e	un-cle pur-ple cod-dle

KEY:
V - vowel
C - consonant
e - silent e
r - controlling r
XX - any two letters
L - the letter l

Important Note:
Teach the vocabulary "consonant" and "vowel" when you teach sounds. This will help your child see the consonant/vowel patterns more easily when you begin to teach new syllables. The syllable pattern determines what the vowel sound should be, this is why syllable patterns matter. The reader should not guess vowel sounds.

34

x

Fox waits for otter in tall grass.

x   fox   /ks/

Closed Syllable

Key Features	• 1 vowel followed by a consonant. • The vowel is short.
Letter Pattern	VC
Vowel Sound	1 short vowel

1 Syllable Words	*2 Syllable Words*
if	den-tist
at	in-sect
mop	cac-tus
stack	sub-tract
math	wind-mill
quest	chop-stick

KEY:
V - vowel
C - consonant

fox

Big buzzes in fox's ear.
Fox runs away.

Closed Syllable

Make your own example words:

C	V	C

C	C	V	C

C	V	C	C

KEY:
V - vowel
C - consonant

I am a READER AWARD

Presented to:

_____

_____ ⭐ _____

Teacher   Date

Did you know? You are a reader!

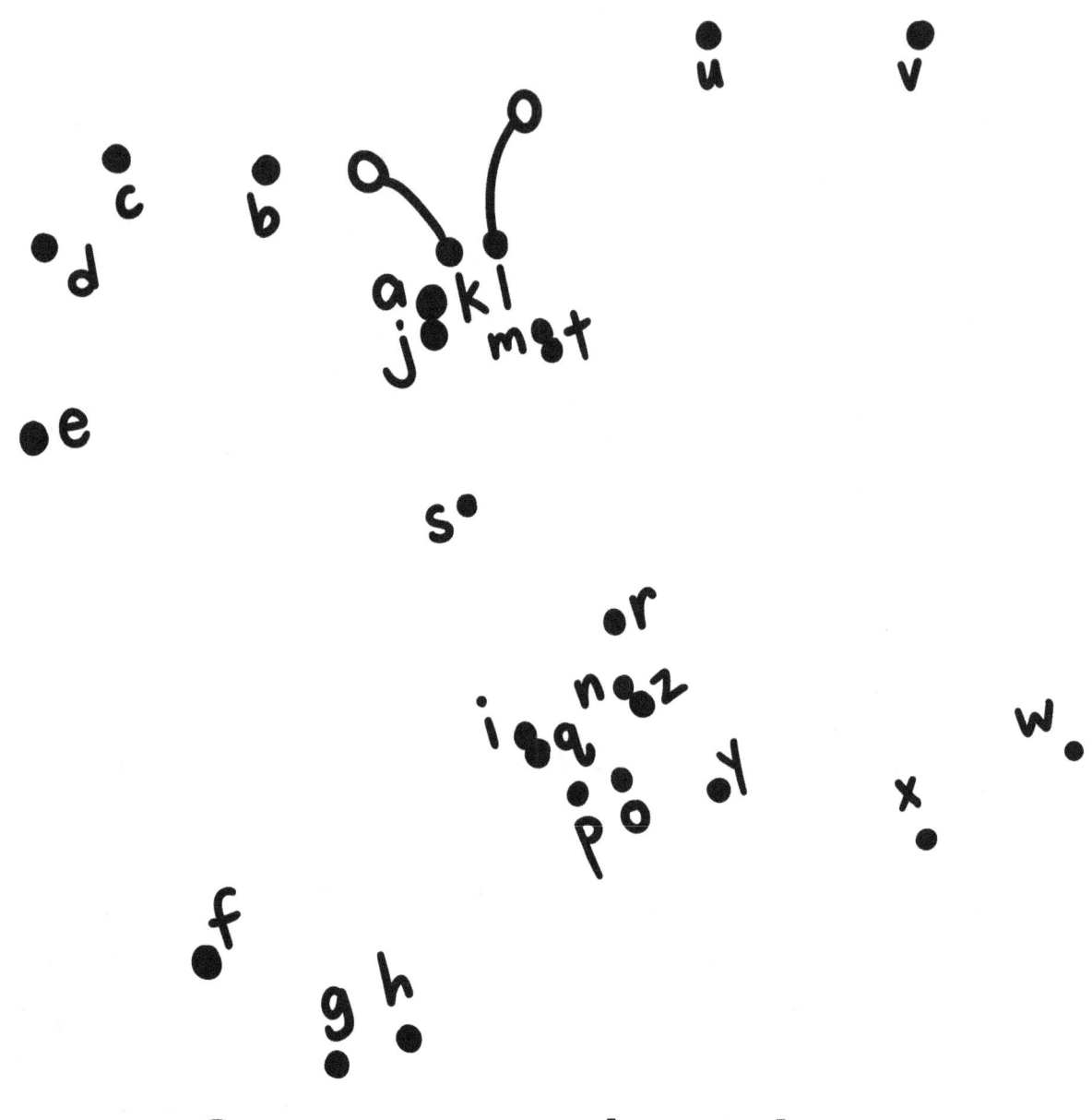

Connect the dots.

Use the alphabet song to connect dots.
Start at lowercase a.

40

qu

Then, Fox stops to watch a yellow quail.

qu   quail   /kw/

Controlled Word Lists
b, a, g, t

at	ab
bat	tab
bag	tat
tag	bab
gab	gag
gat	bag

j

Fox jumps out of the grass,
scaring the quail.

j   jump   /j/

Sound Games

Find & Seek
- ★ **Parent:** *Find something that has the (or starts with) a /k/.*
- ★ **Parent:** Give a countdown.
- ★ **Child:** Runs and finds an object that starts with the sound.

Mystery Bag
- ★ **Parent:** Put small toys (or plastic letters) in a bag and ask the child to pull out 1 toy at a time.
- ★ **Parent:** *What is this?*
- ★ **Child:** *Cow.*
- ★ **Parent:** *C-ow starts with /k/. Say /k/.*
- ★ **Child:** */k/*
- ★ **Parent:** *What says /k/?*
- ★ **Child:** *"k" or "c"*

Hop Sounds
- ★ **Parent:** *Say 'map.'*
- ★ **Child:** *Map.*
- ★ **Parent:** *Let's hop the number of sounds in 'map.'*
- ★ **Parent:** Grab child's hand to guide hopping.
- ★ **Parent/Child:** */m/ hop, /a/ hop, /p/ hop*
- ★ **Parent:** *What word did we hop?*
- ★ **Child:** *Map.*

I spy
- ★ **Parent:** *I spy something that starts with a /k/.*
- ★ **Child:** *Cat!*

Play
Sound Scavenger Hunt!

Say a letter sound. Find objects with the same beginning sound.

Controlled Word Lists
b, a, g, t, s, i, p

tab	tag
bat	tip
pat	sip
pit	gab
sap	bag
gas	pig
big	pigs
bit	tags
sit	bags
sat	bass

d

A brown dog barks
at the snake in a tree.

d   dog   /d/

Controlled Word Lists
k, c, f, o, x, qu, j

cab	fog
bat	top
bot	quip
fix	jab
fax	jog
tax	cot
jig	pot
quit	pots
kit	quits
cap	kiss

e

A nest with many eggs
is hidden in the tree.

e   egg   /e/

Choosing Early Literacy Tools

Below is a checklist of questions to ask when choosing a new early literacy tool or curriculum.

- ☐ Does the tool emphasize sound/letter correspondence? Effective approaches teach 3-5 sounds at a time until mastery.

  - ☐ Via being shown the printed letter first (print to speech)

  - ☐ Via being given the spoken sound first and match to a printed letter (speech to print)

- ☐ Does the tool avoid teaching sight words as "whole words" until the reader masters all basic alphabet sounds?

- ☐ Does the tool use "sound it out" as the main verbal prompt to encourage the early reader when reading and spelling?

- ☐ Does the tool encourage pointing at the word to help focus eyes and attention?

- ☐ Does the tool encourage guessing of sight word lists, irregular words, or high-frequency words?*

  *Instead of allowing guessing, we should read high frequency irregular words (due to not yet being taught all the rules of reading) for our reader.

- ☐ Does the tool encourage reading *aloud* in safe spaces, free from auditory and visual distractions?

n

Night slowly settles on the garden.

n night /n/

Alphabetic Principle vs. Sight Words

Sight words are the outcome of effective reading instruction and should not be the focus of the process.

Many children learn to guess by focusing on reading whole words without mastering basic decoding (or sounding out) skills. Sight words become locked in a child's brain when a child eventually learns to recognize a word rapidly and automatically *due to repeated decoding practice*. Early readers should not memorize words as if they were a picture, which is what most "sight word instruction" looks like today. For most young children, focusing on sight word instruction or memorizing lists of common words is not the best approach to teaching reading.

In contrast, the alphabetic principle teaches early readers to pay attention to each letter and associate letters with sounds that form words.

den

The garden animals return to dens.
A den is where an animal lives.

Play

Sound Hopscotch!

Say the correct sound as you jump
on each box or boxes.

r

It's time for a break.
Do you like to run outside?

r run /r/

Controlled Word Lists
d, e, n, r, l

dab	fed
lab	led
dot	ten
red	ill
lax	bed
tad	quill
dig	loss
net	less
kid	bill
rap	dill

I

Go outside.
Find, draw, or trace the leaf.

I   leaf   /l/

Spelling

If your early reader is developing the fine motor skills for a pencil or traditional writing tool, consider using letter tiles or magnets to teach spelling. Spelling is a separate skill from handwriting.

Teach your child to sound words out one sound at a time to spell.

Dictate practice words from the controlled wordlists in this coloring book that your reader can comfortably read. Model sounding out as spelling.

If your reader struggles with identifying the correct spelling for sounds, your reader may need to work on their "speech to print skills."

Easy Sample Script:

   ★ **Parent:** *Say "cat."*
   ★ **Child:** *Cat.*
   ★ **Parent:** *Sound it out as you spell.*
   ★ **Child:** Says /k/ and writes "c" or "k" (encourage the child to ask if the word is spelled with a c or k if they are unsure)
   ★ **Child:** Says /a/ writes "a"
   ★ **Child:** Says /t/ writes "t"

Sound it out as you spell.

<u>Guess the word!</u>

Challenge your reader to draw objects
that start with the sound /____/.

h

Big explores a hill
behind the garden.

h   hill   /h/

a
e
i
o
u

Stretch the vowel when blending.

U

Big flies up the hill.

u up /u/

A Reading Chant

I'm smart!

I'm a reader.

No one

can take that away from me.

I keep

My calm

And sound words out

Loud, loud, loud!

I stretch the sounds.

Stretch the sounds.

Then listen carefully...

To set

The words

Free.

m

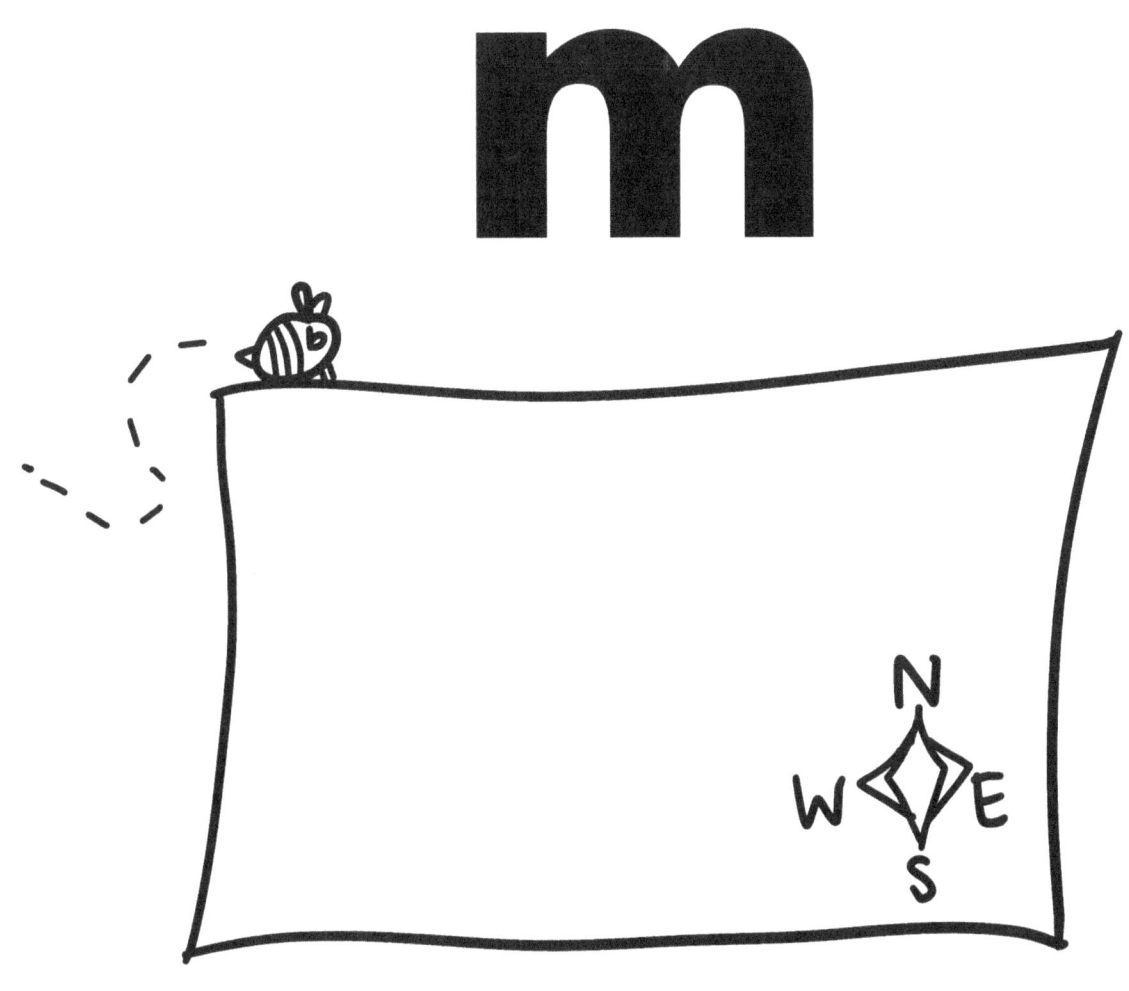

Draw a garden map.
What does Big see from the hilltop?

m   map   /m/

A Letter from Mom to Me:

This is an example letter. Use this letter to inspire and prepare you to write your own letter.

Dear child of mine.

Dear reader and future helper

Leader

Problem solver

You can read!

Reading gives you power

reading is a superpower that can never be taken away,

locked inside of you

Treasure the sound of letters.

Always with my love,

Your mom

hum

Big, the bumblebee,
hums as he explores.

A Letter from Parent to Child:

Write your own letter to inspire your reader, now or in the future.

DATE: _____

DEAR _____,

_____

_____

_____

_____

_____

WITH LOVE,

_____

V

A thick watermelon vine
grows down the hill.

v   vine   /v/

KEEP CALM and SOUND WORDS OUT

W

The vine ends in front of a
water well.

w   well   /w/

Color the b's.

Discover the hidden image by shading the parts labeled with a lowercase b.

What words starts with /b/?

z

Big buzzes
in the sound garden all day.

z buzz /z/

Controlled Word Lists
h, u, m, v, w, z, y

mug	yak
hug	zap
hot	zip
hit	yip
fun	zen
vex	mud
wig	jazz
wet	fuzz
him	buzz
cup	cuff

y

Big is tired. He yawns as he rests in the sound garden.

y   yawn   /y/

Appendix

Reading Action Plan

WHO?	
WHEN?	
WHERE?	
TOOLS/ STRATEGIES?	
FOCUS SOUNDS?	

Extended Scope and Sequence

The Basic Code

Use the basic code on the next page to teach your child 3-5 sounds at a time. Teach consonant digraphs after you teach one sound per alphabet letter. Teach the concept - "short vowels" and "consonants." Using sounding out loud strategies, teach your child to blend these sounds together into CVC words.	Short vowels (a, e, i, o, u)
	Consonants (b-z)
	Consonant digraphs (ch, th, wh, ck, sh)

Early Blending

Using sounding out loud strategies, teach your child to blend these special sounds together.	Consonant blends, no new sounds (br, mp, cl, st, dr, etc)
	Glued sounds (am, an all)
	Glued sounds (-ng/-nk sounds)

Suffixes & Silent e

Using sounding out loud strategies, teach your child to blend these special sounds together. Teach what is a syllable, baseword, and suffix.	Baseword/Suffix -s/-es
	Silent e syllable (long vowels) Syllable
	High frequency words

More Sounds & Syllables

Using sounding out loud strategies, teach your child to blend these special sounds together. Teach any new concepts, including word types and syllables.	R-controlled vowels/syllable
	Vowel teams (ai, ay, ee, ey, etc) Homophones
	2-Syllable words Compound words

Final Sounds & Syllables

Using sounding out loud strategies, teach your child to blend these special sounds together. Teach any new concepts, including word types and syllables.	Consonant-le syllable
	Open syllable
	Common prefixes/suffixes (-ed, -ing, un-, re-) Additional sounds (y as a vowel, ph, etc)

PARTS OF A BOOK TRACKER

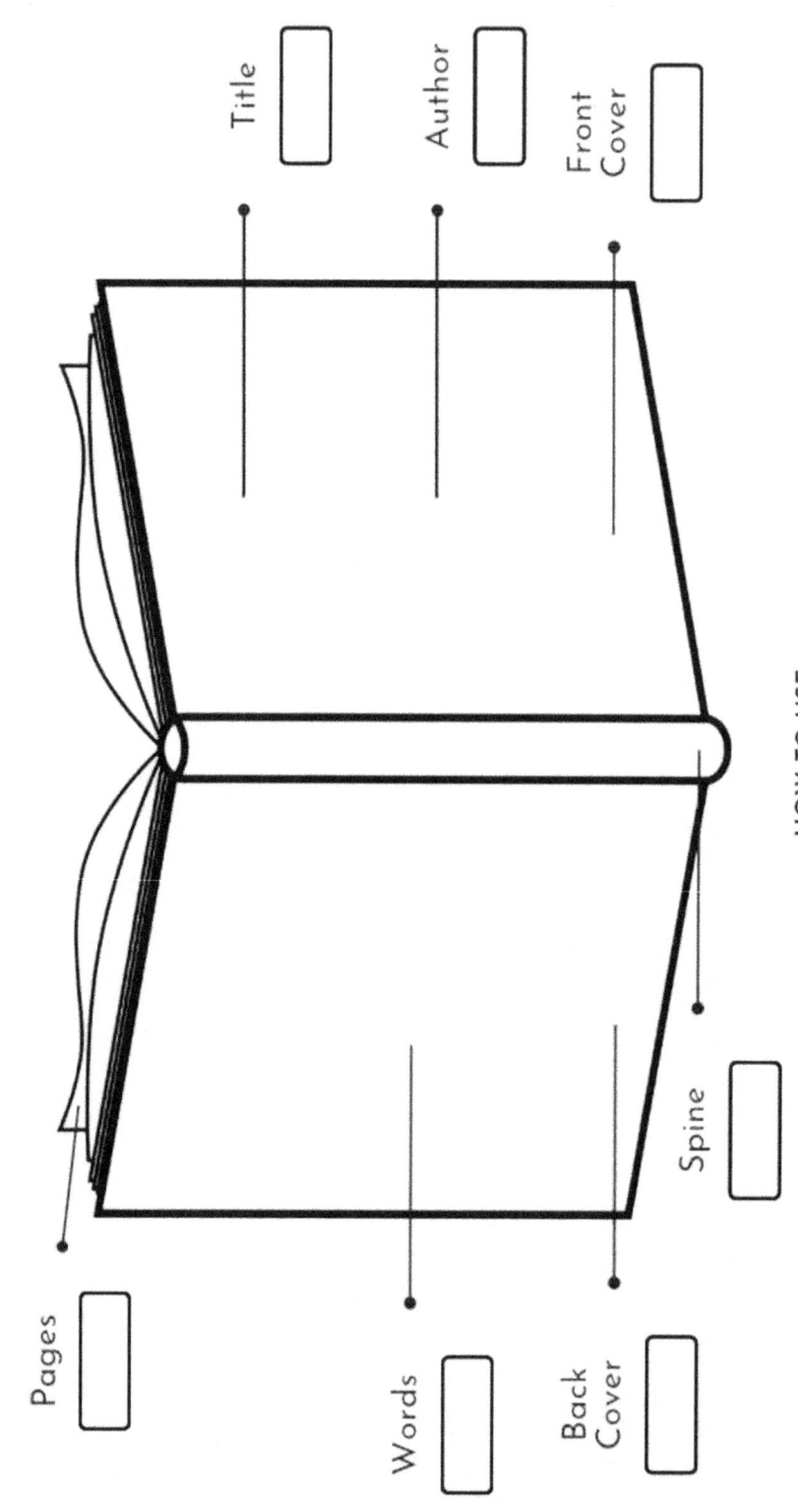

Title

Author

Front Cover

Pages

Words

Spine

Back Cover

HOW TO USE:

Teach your child the parts of the book.
Draw a picture of their favorite book on the blank book above.

Tell early readers to always put books away with the spine out. Make sure they orient the book right side up. This will help them pay attention to how letter symbols are oriented.

Always point to the words as you read them. For very early readers this helps them understand the story is coming from the letter symbols on the page, also called "words."

Online Resources

There are many free or low-cost online tools and resources available for families. Parents can easily get trained on how to teach a reader through structured literacy. Structured literacy is a systematic approach to teaching early readers that ensures a reader demonstrates mastery of skills before advancing. No matter what resources you use, start with the understanding that structured literacy is how <u>all</u> children can be taught to read.

I am here to help. If you want support teaching an early reader, you can also get instructional coaching, tutoring, and free printable resources from a homeschool mom + dyslexia tutor at <u>School.ReadingGardenClub.com</u>. Reach out if you cannot find a resource to meet your reader where they are.

Your Reading Teacher,
Elisabeth Forde, M.Ed.

1. **Reading Garden Club School** offers free printables and resources designed for Parents, including sound cards, decodables readers can illustrate, an early reading glossary for Parents, and new tools updated every month.
   [https://school.readinggardenclub.com]

2. Bookmark **ReadingRockets.org**. This extensive website has videos and free self-paced training on what effective structured literacy instruction looks like.
   [https://readingrockets.org]

3. The **UFLI Parent Hub** links many free literacy resources. I recommend the University of Florida Literacy Institute Instructor's manual for serious Parents that want to provide structured literacy reading instruction. All instructional resources are free for anyone to download and print.
   [https://ufli.education.ufl.edu/resources/parent/]

4. The **Cox Campus video courses for educators** are focused on structured literacy and parents can take the free training.
   [https://learn.coxcampus.org/tracks/k-3/]

5. Explore your local **public library**'s digital and physical resources. Libraries offer literacy events for children, online subscriptions, and so much more. Talk directly with your children's librarian about what resources they have available for engaging your reader's interests.

PARTS OF A PAGE TRACKER

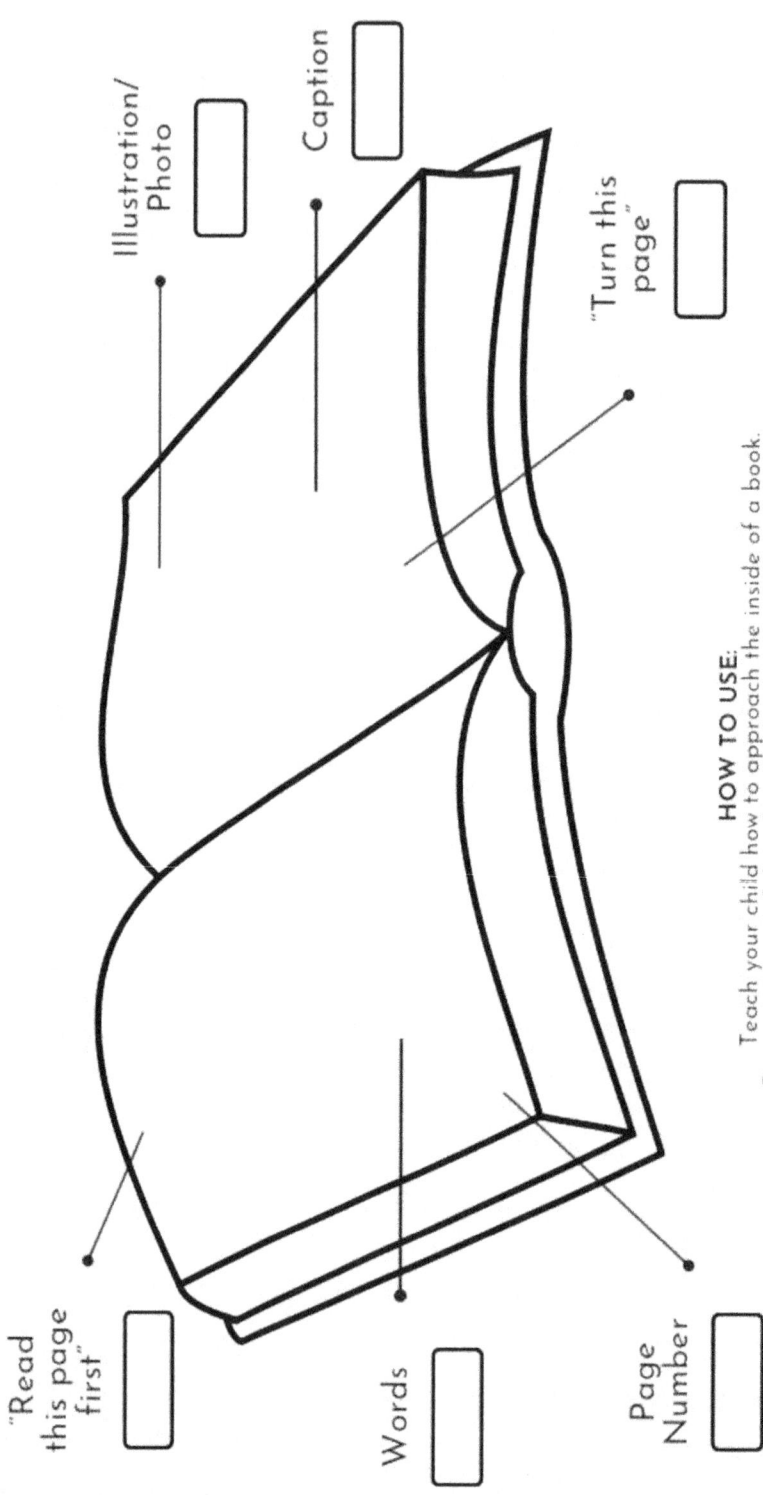

Illustration/
Photo

Caption

"Turn this
page"

"Read
this page
first"

Words

Page
Number

HOW TO USE:

Teach your child how to approach the inside of a book.
Draw a picture of their favorite book on the blank book above.

Tell early readers to always read the left page first. Make sure they orient the book right side up. This will help them pay attention to
how letter symbols are oriented.

Always point to the words as you read them. For very early readers this helps them understand the story is coming from the letter
symbols on the page, also called "words." Ask your early reader to help you turn pages.

Sound Cards

a

Big sits on an apple.

a apple /a/

b

Big is a bumblebee.

b bumblebee /b/

c

Kids chase a cat around the pond.

c cat /k/

d

A brown dog barks
at the snake in a tree.

d dog /d/

e

A nest with many eggs
is hidden in the tree.

e egg /e/

f

The green fish swims in the pond.

f fish /f/

g

A girl eats the apple.

g girl /g/

h

Big explores a hill
behind the garden.

h hill /h/

i

Big also has an iguana friend.

i iguana /i/

j

Fox jumps out of the grass,
scaring the quail.

j jump /j/

k

Kids play in the sound garden.

k kids /k/

l

Go outside.
Find, draw, or trace the leaf.

l leaf /l/

Sound Cards

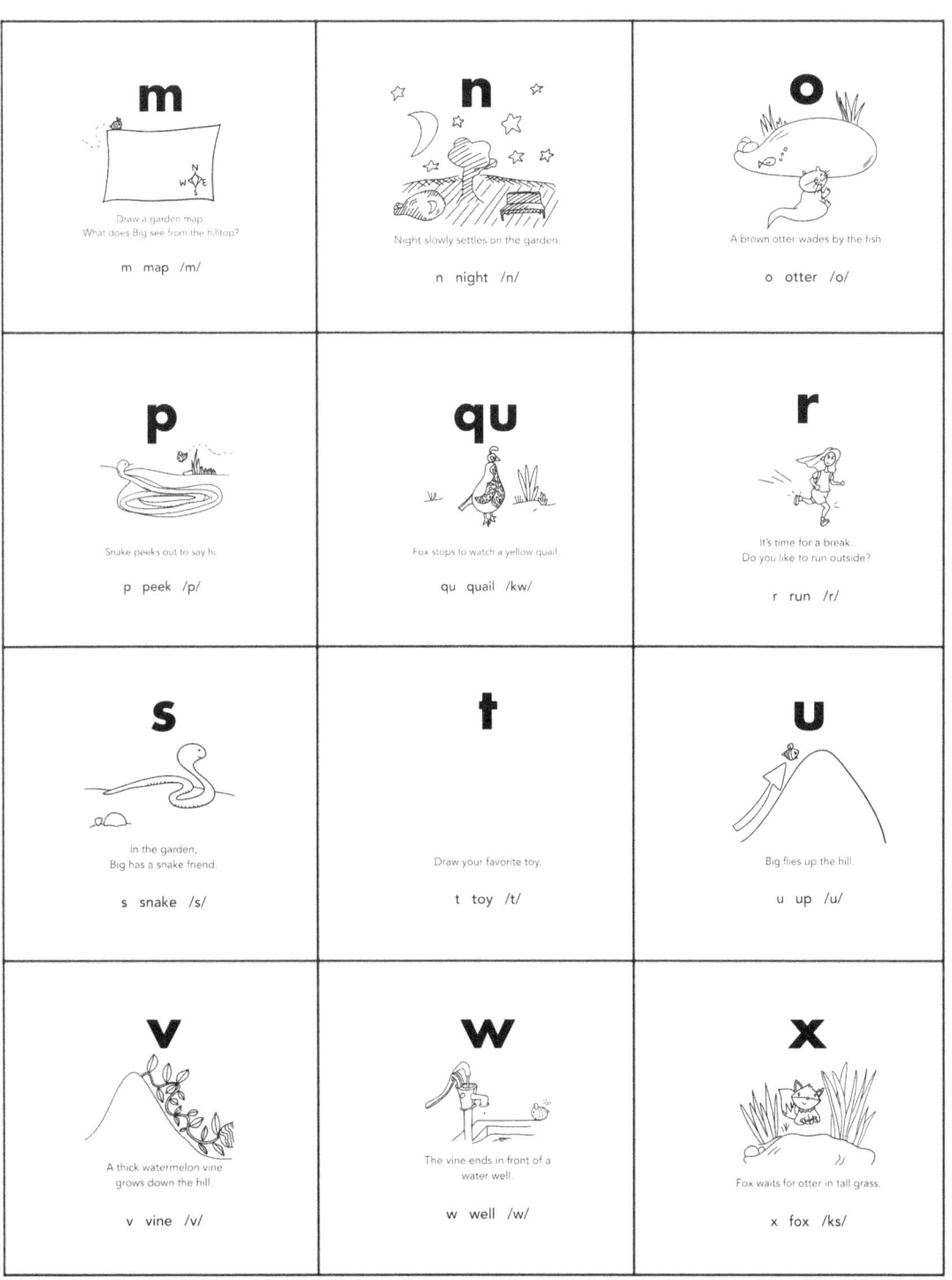

m Draw a garden map. What does Big see from the hilltop? m map /m/	**n** Night slowly settles on the garden. n night /n/	**o** A brown otter wades by the fish. o otter /o/
p Snake peeks out to say hi. p peek /p/	**qu** Fox stops to watch a yellow quail. qu quail /kw/	**r** It's time for a break. Do you like to run outside? r run /r/
s In the garden, Big has a snake friend. s snake /s/	**t** Draw your favorite toy. t toy /t/	**u** Big flies up the hill. u up /u/
v A thick watermelon vine grows down the hill. v vine /v/	**w** The vine ends in front of a water well. w well /w/	**x** Fox waits for otter in tall grass. x fox /ks/

Sound Cards

y Big is tired. He yawns as he rests in the sound garden. y yawn /y/	**z** Big buzzes in the sound garden all day z buzz /z/	

About the Author + Illustrator

My name is Elisabeth Forde. I am a dyslexia tutor with 10+ years of experience utilizing "science of reading" research-based methods. I teach reading skills to all ages including adults, but my passion and the majority of my experience is with young children with learning differences. I taught at the elementary, middle, and high school levels as a classroom teacher and special educator in American public schools. I also taught English online and abroad to foreign students and teacher preparation courses at the graduate level. Currently, I consult as an online instructional coach and privately tutor children with disabilities.

I love reading and sharing my love of reading with others!

Join my mailing list for freebies + updates.